Self Help

Self Help

A Guide for the Retiring

Elizabeth Poreba

RESOURCE *Publications* · Eugene, Oregon

SELF HELP
A Guide for the Retiring

Resource Publications
An Imprint of Wipf and Stock Publishers
199 W. 8th Ave., Suite 3
Eugene, OR 97401

www.wipfandstock.com

PAPERBACK ISBN: 978-1-5326-1975-5
HARDCOVER ISBN: 978-1-4982-4631-6
EBOOK ISBN: 978-1-4982-4630-9

Manufactured in the U.S.A.

Acknowledgements

Boomer Lit: "Fissures" and "Tourists"

Canary: "February Thaw"

Ducts: "Yellow-Crowned Night Heron"

Journal of Feminist Studies in Religion: "Feast of St. Philip"

Limestone: "A Walk in the Back Lot"

Mom Egg Review: "Passed On"

Mudfish: "Feast of the Holy Guardian Angels"

Time of Singing: "Beethoven's Violin Concerto in D Major, Op. 61"

Written River: "*Verde Que Te Quiero Verde*"

Among the many indignities of aging is the irresistible temptation to reach for some menu of bromides and convey to the world those invaluable lessons about living.

—Laura Kipnis

Contents

III.

I

Fissures

I'm made of words mostly.
The rest is thin.

Words hold me up
like bones beneath the skin.

The thought of a soul within
is *mute* or *moot*

and slides in a vowel shift
from silent to irrelevant.

Perhaps such accidents
of sound are not mere

motions of the tongue.
I ponder them as seers once

studied fissures in burned bone.

Leaving Thessaloniki

I would leave, but the farmers have closed the airport.
      Besides, they have a story around here
      About a mother and daughter parting
      And it doesn't turn out well
      From the mother's point of view.

They have circled the airport with their green tractors,
      And they look like reliable men,
      Worried like their saints.
      Why should they pay taxes?
      These changes are probably not for the better.

I would leave if they opened the airport,
      Though how fair is it that I
      Should go and never know
      The color of the tight buds
      I first saw a week ago?

I would leave, but I can't.
      Why should we part, anyway?
      Farmers here keep their families close.
      They build walls around their compounds
      And include chickens and a vegetable garden.

Sundays, I'd set a table outside,
      We'd eat and listen to the chickens mutter
            About the boredom of staying together.

Sister Ghost

for Gertrude Tredwell of 29 East 4ᵀᴴ Street, 1840–1933

In the favored front room, in Father's bed,
windows papered to keep out cold,
she lay ready *to die to the Kingdom*
as she'd been told, propped on feathers plucked
from geese of bygone feasts, remembering
the great china platter, grace intoned
before meals, also perhaps graces
she had missed, the drapes always drawn
to spare the furniture from the sun.

It was hers at the last, the stately parlor,
the marble stoop pocked by coal ash,
the triple friezes belting the high ceilings
and the columns on Father's fine wardrobe,
temple to the camphor-scented topcoat,
the opera hat and folded cravats.
Even when the charming nephew died
she continued to preside, imperial,
object of rumors of wealth and madness,
living past the money until rot took the walls
and soot shadowed the plaster work.

Now I, the smiling docent, guard
the fine red Rococo parlor set
where she and her sisters sat for life
waiting for the maid to light the fire.
I watch the sun touch the carpet square
as it did in her day at the same hour,

waiting boxed in her house, hard-pressed
against the tenements, even
the Ladies' Mile gone, a thread pulled uptown.

The tourists depart. The house hunches,
its fanlight flutters, its pillars brace
like shoulders tensed above the street.
It is the hour for Gertrude to appear
and wait with me until it's time
to close the shutters and take in the sign.
We sit, straight backs scarcely touching
our chairs, two ladies about to disappear
like the house, holding tight
to our consequence, despite
accumulating evidence.

Feast of St. Phillip

Fellow literalist, your doubt
  about the loaves and fishes
    always comforted me.

When you responded to His return
  from death with your
    over-the-top request to see more

and were rebuked—
  Don't you know me?—
    you had my sympathy.

Maybe knowing Greek got you in.
  God knows how you translated
    what you could scarcely understand,

but God, we're told, draws straight
  with crooked lines, a relief to us both,
    good with words, but at the wrong times.

Hear my prayer, Philip,
  fifth of the twelve. Your gaze suggests
    disquiet can be stilled.

Aubade

"Modern longevity . . . .presents a new challenge to marriage."

I would like to march downstairs where you are eating Cheerios
and watching the NBC Morning News to inform you that
an out-of-tune crow is terrorizing the neighborhood.

As you grind your coffee beans, I would like to remark that
the rain keeps promising a comeback then sighs
and disappears behind a cloud cover.

I would like to ask you, *What's up? Does that crow have a hook in its gut?*
His situation seemed dramatic, but the other crows only croak *nownownow,*
as you've been known to do.

Whitman's widowed mocking-bird mourned his mate in melody,
and the swan's cry of loss moved Valmiki to lyric poetry,
but right now I could be that crow causing a ruckus,

and I'd like to ask you, what about this?

The Boxer at the Met

The artist limed his wounds with care
     and swelled his cauliflower ear.

It's a brief interval between bouts.
     He looks back. Who's out?

Resting his elbows on his knees,
     hunching, bulky, an abject beast.

Once people stroked his feet for luck,
     leaving the unguent of their touch.

Invaded, Romans buried him deep.
     Dirt chewed him brown and verdigris.

Now he's earth and art enmeshed,
     his bronze friable as flesh.

Around him, the standing statues pose
     silent as stone dolls,

But this one crouching, close to defeat,
     suffering, seems to speak.

Retiring the Red Pen

I no longer got their jokes. I confused Celina with Cecily and Selin,
Sean and Shané, Jane and Janay, Jenna and Jana.
There was a year when Sofia, Safyah, and Susa sat together.
Liam, Ian, Nina, Lena, Liana. Two Mildreds and an Azalea.
Never a Huck, but a Finn and a Cameron, some Jacksons and a Jan.
A very tall Abraham. Several Sarahs.
Abram, Hannah, Hamza, Jacob, Jakob, Mahmoud, Mo—
who cares who did their homework now?
Elijah, Jeremiah, Isaiah, Moses,
an Eve, Evas, Steves, Jesus, Jesús,
Treashure, Precious, Charm.
Nina and Ian. Kinga.
A non-Linnean system: each name denotes a kingdom.
Thirty-six years of singularities,
Isabelles, Isabellas, Averies.
MIa, MAya, MYa,
Mine only now in memory.
The wealth of nations through my fingers:
Tiara, Amber, Golda, Ebony.

On Being Asked "How are you?"

Since you ask, I'm tired of being invisible, in conversation, a polite inquiry not to be answered at length, on the street, a mild presence, unremarkable—

And now here's June also about to become invisible, subject to selective memory, such as, *That June, when the baby was afraid of escalators* or *when the peas were scarce*—

Meanwhile a leaf progresses along the brook, its future disappearance leaching substance from the moment, the brook flashes in the sun, rushing to lose itself into the Hudson—

And the baby can't quite catch the ball no matter how carefully I throw, and when he can, where will I—who am even now mostly invisible, hazy—

My Condition

I.

I must stay quiet today.
I must take time to consider my situation.

Not that what's inside is dark so much as
petty, gnawing and querulous.

The sun is up again, time to turn off the desk lamp,
coffee, day ahead, blank slate.

I will bring paper to the porch
and take notes, perch on a bench

and call myself to account, muse on ruses
necessary to maintain my vacancy.

No more temporizing about the trees,
their flowering, their winter shadows,

no more letting the shapes and habits of trees,
or stories of characters moved by passion,

or any creature's unaccountable need for action
distract me from the pathos of my condition.

II.

Called by monks *acedie*:
the beast that stalked
their souls at midday.

Familiar, close to ease
but without energetic
preliminaries, from the start
no get up and go,
just no.

A thick fog on every
horizon, a flat path
looping back, no detour
to be sought, because worse
would be to be lost.

As winter protects
root and pith,
so do I,
languid with this disease,
reject attempts
at remedies.

III.

Peonies bloomed beyond the strength of their stems,
fabulous flowers prone,
                  collapsed balloons.

What a waste, all that furl and layering now abject,
spent, just too much,
                  overblown effect.

But they're not brown-edged yet,
so it's time to cut these and crowd them all
                  for one final folderol.

Break

Myself   water wishing to be
still   a quiet room
flowers   holding steady
no evidence as yet   of decay
the clock   coming around.

If you   would just
arrive   bustle at the airport, traffic
the door,   just stay
you   this room,
one entire   evening.

If you   would just sit,
not break   away
as ice   breaks
with a terrific crack.

The More We Are Ourselves,
The Less Self in Us

A formation or flash mob brought on

      by the angle of the wind or sun,

pigeons east up 6th Street, each an oscillation,

         a flutter in the larger helter-skelter

         circling, falling upward together

               enacting one true bird nature
feeding later on pizza crusts,

      warbling love on pavements,

perching low for fear of the hawk.

             Now another one
by the window in free fall

      after the long sound of its solo wing plow

      it veers back to the gang—

Gems

Gleam or
glister:

no word
can match

this hard
horde's luster.

Cut to catch
light: mineral

suns pried
out of dirt

honed to
look sharp.

Parts of the first
spark just

like us:
radiance

unlikely thrust,
cosmic dust.

Passed On

Another baby, my DNA cunningly packaged, his little cap covering poten-
tial crackpot notions, those eyes ready to marvel at sunsets, the mirror.

Another object of my daughter's attention, fewer phone calls for me;
for her, stacks of drink boxes, tears, emergency room visits, fears of strang-
ers, something in the closet.

Here on my desk, a friend's amused face peers from her memorial program.

At the service, her hirsute heirs looked sad enough but avid, I could tell, to
shed their suits, get back to tinkering with the planet's chemistry

and leave their grandmother to sift away quietly.

Beethoven's Violin Concerto in D Major, Op. 61

Fashioned though seeming inevitable, devised within form yet beyond form,
stretching form just so to a place impossible to dwell in,
it rends him, he must grip the doorframe to keep his heart from breaking.

Maybe when the heart cracks, spirit pours out, and this is spirit's evidence,
like the evidence lately found for the particle named for Higgs or God,
that turns out to be essential, giving mass as spirit gives life.

Retiring Is Not Retreating

Think of the snail
and its portable lair
that is convenient for naps
and solitude, slowing it down
but not impeding its silver progress.

Though that foot flips
back to become portcullis,
the plan is still going forward,
as the snail dwells deaf to the world
in a spiral shell that experience swells.

You always were the retiring
type. Now it's condoned, you're
on your own. No meetings mandated,
unless maybe for mating. Soft going, slide on.

II

Letter to a Distant Daughter

The surplus meaning is infinite here.—Basho

A funny thing I had thought
to mention:

I finally found my slippers,
tossed like abandoned orphans,

and I was unreasonably glad
as if they were important.

It was a small joke on me,
a cheerful thing

that I had planned to tell you
—with maybe a laugh—

but you would have thought
She has nothing much to say

besides this little story.

Moisés and Nicholas

In the lot where the sushi place blew up,
someone outlined two graves in white rocks,
propped an angel facing east on each, and decked
the fence with photos of the two lost.

Out of red chalk, less earth than brick dust,
a strange weed has asserted a phalanx of straight stems
bearing brown leaves and berries too dry
to feed the sparrows.

The fence, of wire looped and galvanized,
segments the sight into soft rhomboids. Close up,
what's within is a blur. I hook fingers
through the spaces wrought

to separate the lucky from the not.

The Parable of the Vineyard

Another murder.
　　　　　　The son, no less.
The vineyard owner did not expect.

Something went awry.
　　　　　　It was not supposed to end this way,
as any parent would say.

Maybe something wrong in the formula,
too much need for more,
scant sense of limits.

Maybe, having lavished beauty over the planet,
　　　　　　the landlord couldn't resist making minds to admire it,
a crazy miscalculation,

beauty's restraint not being to human taste.
　　　　　　Yet they say
God doesn't make mistakes.

A Good Rain

A good, soaking rain Mother always said
and would have said tonight
as garden roots ease their grip
and leaves cup to hold the drops.

A good soak she'd say, as if
she could quench her thirst in it
from the front porch with her cigarette.

It never rains but I hear her voice,
its memory like a melodic line
flowing as music does in time,
real only as time is,

which is not, but liable to be caught
like a leaf in the eddy of a brook, lodged
only long enough to look.

Stern

As the magnolia,
stricken in one night,

its brassy leaves
all in a heap,

saves a few
furred catkins

to make it to spring,
she kept her joys

secret, most gripping
the high branches

away from the coming
hungry deer.

Style

Mother's was casual, even
in the face of heavy weather.

When she left the windows open in '38
she saved the summer cottage—

The storm just blew through!

Her movies featured pilots and their last cigarettes
before nonchalantly taking off to bomb Germany.

She smiled, *If I'd known I'd live so long,
I'd have taken better care of myself—*

Gone without complaint, as the fading garden
lies down after late summer rain.

Perspective

If some foreign, hunted company
should happen upon our property

and seek refuge in this safety
that has become so burdensome to me,

they might find cover in the barn.

     From there, they might gaze around

     at the signs of our prosperity,
     at the garden where berries weigh

     their canes and vines splay,
     and imagine that we spend our days

     in tranquility, and that our lamps,
     come night, release

     light in golden rectangles,
     perfect ratios of peace.

Afternoon Nap

Nothing to do, nothing to do or say,
not the day for groceries or the library,
coffee cups in disarray,
magazines and hats, bug spray,
let it all stay, let the place
go to pot with the unwound clocks—

There's us in a little boat,
Let's cut the motor and ride out the storm, I shout
but wake alone, the wind seething about,
insisting that I head to shore, where rocks
wait and sea spits fast at my shaky craft
and you pace with running figures on the sand,
a rope I can not hope to catch in your hand—

The Land of Shades Gives Birth

A copse after the sun-scalded meadow
or a cave. Chill of shadow. The skin
senses something like nothing
but it is not.

Light leaches from between the trees,
the mouth of the cave draws shut.
Noises unnamable. Not true to say
this is nothing.

Something, yes. What is left
after the eye parses. The selvedges
that seemed meaningless
at the time.

The shades are thick with these
forgotten, unshapely fragments
and could, yes, *give birth.*

California Light

Even in this darkened room, even with closed eyes,
light off the Pacific pierces the edge of the shade
and penetrates, making itself known by the moving shadows
of the leaves, a cool light, intellectual, probing, indifferent.

Indifferent, I complain and think how old light is,
an old idea always making itself new, and I think
I am old like my father was and like him always
forgetting and thinking I'm as new as this light.

Where Were the Dogs in Eden?

Of those succeeding Adam out of dust,
one dog would have been enough,

just one Labrador necessary,
then no radical rib-ectomy.

Mr/Ms Dust could have remained
undifferentiated, self-contained—

no apple eating, no regrets,
calm androgyny, no sex, no death.

Watch one leashed to a parking meter,
naked as God made him, patient waiter,

expressive tail, hopeful eyes
okay with his bit part, still

a fan of this enterprise.

February Thaw

Light's love for water, sentimental
in rainbows, harsh here, glinting,
the brook's white thread become lava,
a tumult, thin and colossal, an aria—

She could be in love or dying,
in a language unknown but the feeling
is familiar, a wave, a leaf
released to the rush,

Snow to liquid, heart to mouth
all transparent—
this moment, her singing,
the waters swelling

and all melting headlong

A Walk in the Back Lot

Criss-crossed by carnage below the trees—
branches tossed and heaped as if
for bonfires of monstrous festivities—
and sealed off by snow annealed to shell,
the wood road was invisible.

I'd gone to get a glimpse of deer whose hoofs
had pocked paths in the debris, to note
signs of lives beside my own, grace notes
to bring home, but got lost instead,
for their wandering led beyond the ridge
to a terrain untouched by sun, edged in pines
that soughed in sounds unknown,

and I was deeply lost, though I'd have thought
these woods were my own.

How Does the Rushing Brook Sound?

I stop on my walk to decide— traffic,
something headlong, a nibbling, a chuckle
or a swallowing—greed or generosity?

Maybe it's the sound of creation at work,
rounding rocks and hills, about to slice
our lawns and spill our houses to the sea,

but I would prefer it to be otherwise,
not so heedless and oblivious of me.

Yellow-Crowned Night Heron

Feet wet in the morning rush, alert to what the tide brings,
he allows me to gaze, holds his head as if to say
Yes, this yellow top-knot, flare of backward flightless feathers,
is strange, but watch. This day will not fail.
But I know that soon generalists will prevail:
crows and rats, gulls in regulation grays and blacks
like humorless Puritans, opportunists preying
on these eccentrics, raiding their guileless nests.
The tides already gather bile,
heedless of his delicate life, his silly headgear,
his call uttered only on ritual occasions.

Split

The macaque has become
a little platter of himself
on the market scale, arms opened
as if inviting the buyer to feast.

Looks like he's dreaming,
legs akimbo, stopped acrobat,
elusive presence in the trees
offering the roil of his innards.

Once purely in the world,
hand fast to the next branch,
scent of fruit, special tang of its rot
heat, lice, rain, all sensation his—

I remember myself, a child,
avid, happy to be held,
hungry and satisfied, a creature
that I recognize now

in the split beast also—

Cozumel

Hello island, lucky in sea breeze and light,
late to electricity, to scooters along the wall
where we, so tall, walk, shod so well.

We trod the shell-paved path to Ixchel's shrine,
we sought sacred sparrows and straw children
that the barren leave behind.

We regret the smallpox, the coral reefs
now paled from waters too warm,
we didn't mean to harm.

We caught your sunset from the pizza place.
It was great, worth the price,
something else to bring home.

Ornamental

The hyperbolic cherries are at it again—
straight trunks, shiny columns, seemingly barkless,

Barkless as the city's post-surgical dogs
who no longer wake the neighbors

Neighborhoods fluorescing with these trees,
bred solely to please

Pleasing pinks layering streets
before retreating to leaf

Leaves that all summer filter sun
to comely shadow fall,

and come Fall, parch in place,
forgetting their youthful

full-of-themselves, when they weren't trees
but flowers groomed to please.

III

Self Help

Take the First Weeks Slowly
Dawns, I'm out already to hear the cicadas still at it and the frog pond's throaty spill into the brook. I go inside when the crows start up. There are many afternoons. I notice variations of sky. Coreopsis blooms where we buried the cat. The wren family's faint chipping in the lilac gets louder in July and then stops in August. We are interested in talking about the rain. Trucks bang up and down the road, and cars carrying people off to work made a sound like *shush, shush.*

Get in Touch with Old Friends
Company's coming and there's no getting around it, so after you dust, remind yourself that this is not your mother coming but your friend, she's not judging, she'll be glad to see you. You're cleaning up to compensate for the marionette lines along your mouth, your withered arms.

Consider Your Good Fortune
Exodus describes manna as *flakes like hoarfrost after the dew evaporates.* The Israelites had to ask what it was. Moses reminded them they had been clamoring for bread and this was it. Because it melted when the sun grew hot, they had to eat it right away, no reserves for the next day. Like retirement.

Plan
Life could become a summer afternoon, a slow swim in a warm lake. I could become another backyard roustabout, part of the greedy gang eying the vegetable garden. The larcenous woodchuck returns. We exchange a long gaze but he gives no clue of what to do next.

Détente

Let's start at the beginning you said,
meaning my feet, pleasant
but incorrect, for, like most,
my beginning was head first—

when I had not yet said a wrong thing
and nobody had failed to get my point
or made it into another point,
like the translator who changed

Schiaparelli's Martian *channels* into *canals,*
causing Lowell to write three books
about the brilliant engineers who lived on Mars,
or the one who forgot that *demand* in French

can be *request* and so foiled a treaty.
Distinctions like this, if not lost
between what I mean and what I say
are gone in the gap between

what I say and what you hear anyway.
We get each other wrong, amend, correct,
and go again. But, right now, let's begin
to end this history of being misunderstood,

starting with the feet. That's good.

Feast of the Holy Guardian Angels

Angels might just be figures of speech, but art has a way of bringing them
to feathery reality, swish of robes, light touch of figurative feet on tessel-
lated marble,

Imagine Mary explaining to Joseph, *There was an angel, but don't take this
literally.*

My days these days cannot be taken literally, *cozy afternoon* for dreary rain,
retired for bone idle, and as for *cocktail hour* —

Back to the angels, irresistible, like gussied-up crossing guards, birds'-eye-
viewing traffic to help even if you don't wait for the light, alert in their
elsewhere to your doings, ready to intercede, here and there a nudge,
sometimes a decision handed down

I'm not making fun of guardian angels, I'm looking for a place to put mine,
somewhere in the vestibule of my interior castle, fragile on the shaky
front table.

The Butterfly Effect

The banality of *beauty*,
strange label for so much,

more than pretty—
its definition stretched

beyond roses and sunsets
to Stendhal's *promise of happiness,*

which can refer to anything
that catches the eye.

Consider the butterfly,
its wings checkered, marbled,

or crenelated, its frieze,
or splotch, or spot,

its compound eyes bobbing
from long antennae,

and its usual bug body bearing
on its back the burden

of being both commonplace
and exquisite, suggesting

the presence of imagination
without limit. No wonder

they say it can, wings
unfurled, move the world.

My Approach

I.

Because it's sloppy along the edges,
able to swallow anything,
derivative of sky,

with a false, bland face,
only an accident of bed-rock tilt,
of mountain run-off and supposed springs,

altogether unknowable and shifty,
I must approach the lake
with rigor and strict measure,

breathing on each third stroke,
a beat not heart-felt,
iambic's almost opposite,

off-kilter, allowing me
to look both ways,
cautious and frugal of air.

II.

From the shore,
you see me
ply straight as
a shuttle.
I'm weaving
from water
my kind of
coherence,
gliding like
a key in
the right lock,
good by to
senescence.

Rest Room

A long time in line. I give the knob a little twist, meant to be polite,
to say Is there someone in there? Why this wait?

The man behind me nods. Through the queue, a disapproving stir.
Wouldn't courtesy require more speed from whoever's in there?

At last, the door cracks, a stout gentleman, suspenders, a cane.
I compose my face to no comment. He catches my eye, but not to explain:

Wait, I forgot something and he turns as if to go back in,
then laughs, acknowledging our shared chagrin,

slipping a grace note, an embellishment
over necessities of the moment.

Seaside

Inland, having a personality,
such an effort, so much to do
even when doing nothing:
lists of preferences, stock phrases,
a trustworthy wardrobe,
favorite slippers, a retinue of habits.

Easier here, where the sea delivers,
in great swells from afar,
gigantic arrivals, silky about the ankles,
then fades back in pure sport,
leaving me among the least,
small fry it can catch and release.

Carlos

We follow his silver flippers
      into a rift and lo! teeming flocks
      in martial order, clouds of creatures,

undulant wall paper, their spawned fry snug
      in a coral garden's
      stone shrubbery.

The occasional tang or tile fish
      meandering alone on some
      errand stops to touch his hand.

At a mouthful of salt, I emerge to gasp
      and watch our breathing tubes,
      so many straws in the wind.

This is nature at its best he tells us later,
      passing out the fruit cups;
      on board, he's banal as sea grass.

Yet I had seen a dogfish slaver at his feet,
      and before him, orderly schools
      criss-cross, docile like us.

Dance

It's time to dance he told me
though we'd never danced before,

and our steps fit together
as covalent atoms tether.

At first I didn't meet his eyes
and let feet perform the courtesies.

I looked around, to show
that this was my choice too,

then I spun from him.
He waited and swirled me back again.

When I wavered, he was deliberate.
Then we switched. It was delicate,

but we had to be two.
Solitary dancing wouldn't do,

nor would it do to dictate
turns we must negotiate.

Anniversary #44

In a predictable release,
each unremarkable leaf
consigns itself to sidewalk slush

through which we lurch, inevitable pair
to treat ourselves to dinner, where
we will marvel that we've lasted so much

longer than anticipated
and concur that variety is overrated.
Life provides such narrow choices:

Subatomically, it's lepton or quark;
at all levels, alternatives are stark.
Though a cell assigned the heart might voice

desire to join the leg's design,
it must take its nature as a sign.
Look at twins separated at birth

who discover when they meet again
they've both married women named Elaine.
Who says variety is worth

the strain? We have another year to digest.
Every morning I will pour
your juice half full, never more.

Sparrow

Three-toed bather in the dust
staking territory in a potted plant,
less than half an ounce, born knowing
its songs, and in that, as in most
the rest, not my counterpart, yet
my familiar, fellow city dweller,
import avid to make a go of it,
connoisseur of crumbs, feaster
from detritus while keeping
an eye out for the hawk, famous
for its lust, though most seasons
no time for brooding, busy about
its business, not too proud to hop,
there under a car, stubby beak stuffed,
cloaked in dun—in ancient Egypt
a glyph meaning small, not
a sound or a subject, but not
nothing at all.

Not Everything Known is Learned

Flamingoes mill in their little yard on pink legs.
Their mid-point ankles look like knees
hinging backwards. Their bodies resemble
feathered footballs trailing orange plumes.

Heads like small balloons bob
on necks like downy ropes looping
and wavering until beaks sip water
then stretch to hold the pose.

When kids clatter into the Seaquarium,
the senior bird faces them,
swerves his side-eyed view to take them in,
and spreads his wings to reveal their black lining

with the bravado of a stalker dressed
in only his raincoat. After the general AHHH,
he tucks his head to a nonexistent shoulder,
looks bashful, then repeats.

Where in his brain between
the wiring for his tiny eyes and beak
was there space for this routine?

Could be he's untaught, there was something
in the children that he caught, some joy that his act
picked up and answered back.

Tourists

That night, we got up every hour
to see the Perseid shower, clearest it had been
in years—not that we had ever looked before,
but this was an event we wanted to witness, as if
being outside in the dark, breathing synched
to those starry descents, would make us participants.

Finally, the sky revealed a few, dim stars.
We put on mud boots and blundered out
in bathrobes. We found a level place to stand,
which scent revealed to be a bed of thyme.
After a while, necks craning, we gazed
long enough to see stars between stars,
but none of them moving. I didn't care;
I hadn't really felt like going out—
the Perseids were something I knew about,
like the Eiffel Tower. You visit just
to make sure it matches the postcards.

Long ago, on Cedar Island, in a sleeping bag
that reeked of old canvas, reclining on lumpy sand,
I saw stars shoot straight all over the sky,
as if to destinations. But that thought did not
occur to me at the time. No thought occurred.
At that time, I was not a tourist, the brightness
sufficed, and I belonged to it.

Verde Que Te Quiero Verde

Yet also I hate it, its ceaseless iterations, its one idea
of chlorophyll, root branch bud leaf flower,
the forsythia heaped, the hyacinths overdressed as ever,

day lilies elbowing yet more green
through last summer's brown mat
that in February looked impenetrable,

and lately the forest flowers, those shysters
attempting to con me into a Victorian swoon,
named for alleged virtues, because humans assume
any green so intricately foliated must cure or bless.

I begin to crave a contrary desert, any good dead space,
concrete, asphalt, a way to walk dry shod on dewy mornings,
a little space that keeps still, away from the tramp
of grass marching back in fascist ranks.

But some nights, my mind's eye scans the garden
bleached by darkness, fending for itself, and something
in me is tender, something wants to tend,
and I worry if it's too cold or if the rain falls too hard.

Root Room

As I uncoil, my bones steady,
opening like a jack knife,
clicking like a rollercoaster uphill;
as I, starting with the tail,
reassemble, and last of all
the neck unfurls;
I raise my arms,
I am alive,
I can bend and get back up,
I am lovely I am
the Dawn Redwood
towering over that hotel
on Houston Street,
living fossil
from Mongolian forests
urban, big success,
offspring in every park.

        If whoever's in charge
        had to choose between me
        and that floral survivor
        and local treasure,
        the decision, I suppose,
        would be in my favor;
        but the tree, raiding the water main
        for root room, expiring sweet
        oxygen from traffic fumes,
        knows more than me
        about resiliency.

A Miracle

. . . by definition, leads to activity—pick up your cot,
throw down your crutch, get back to work—
        it is transitory, a flare.

Our friend's home from the hospital,
acting like himself and eating dinner,
        and it's enough, tonight, that he's here.

Like the sea Christ quieted that resumed its rumpus,
the sweet moments we pass shrink back
        to blank stares;

shy as a bird known only by its song,
the miraculous doesn't stay around
        for you to see that it was there.

That this elevator full of bodies,
jostled, distracted but grimly prepared,
        made it at last to the lobby

to spill its passengers into morning air
is also amazing, so you might say
        that miracles are everywhere.

Forecast

The spring after we're gone, the raspberries we coddled through summer
will gallop over the grass, potent with the energy we poured into their
survival.

Cavalries of horseradish will overtake the asparagus, which will raise
a few spears to gaze over the abandoned season.

Harsh-scented catmint will sprawl like conquering soldiers in unkempt
clumps over the luxury of our double-dug beds.

The garlic onion I unearthed for decades will replicate and overwhelm
our perennials' pretty compositions with its scrawny mass production.

The whole garden will follow nature's rule, *Everything in excess*,
including our surprise at our disappearance.

Tompkins Square Park

Though Sanitation's stench almost blots
the light-scented lindens, its din drowning

skateboard rattle and chatter of children,
it's possible to sense, among detritus and flowers,

powers that dote on life in any shape—
weed, crocodile, crackpot, saint—

and, though we may shrink, we can choose to think
that things torn apart will become composed;

that we are right to cherish the running dog,
the blue beds, the babies gazing dumbstruck

from strollers, the elms fenced as if needing restraint;
to feel, in the air between our stories, a force

not quite us, with which we co-create
the swings, the walkways, the curving benches.

Notes

"Aubade" : quote from *Commonweal* "Sex Marriage, and the Church"

"*The Boxer* at the Met" "Since its discovery on the Quirinal Hill of Rome in 1885 near the ancient Baths of Constantine, the statue *Boxer at Rest* has astonished and delighted visitors . . . " Metropolitan Museum of Art Bulletin, June 2013

"*The More We Are Ourselves, the Less Self in Us*": quote from Meister Eckhart

"*The Land of Shades Gives Birth*": Isaiah 26: 19

"*Verde Que Te Quiero Verde*": title from Lorca